A WYOMING STATE OF MIND

ALSO BY THE AUTHOR

Poetry
Prairie Parcels

Children's
C is for Cowboy: A Wyoming Alphabet
Inside the Clown
Falling Stars
V is for Venus Flytrap: A Plant Alphabet
Little Wyoming
Four Wheels West: A Wyoming Number Book
My Teacher Dances on the Desk
Dee and the Mammoth
The Magic Box
Angel's Landing
Booger
Is It True?

Middle Grade
Wedge of Fear
Snap
Secret of the Black Widow, reprint TBA

A WYOMING STATE OF MIND

EUGENE M. GAGLIANO
Wyoming Poet Laureate

Crystal Publishing, LLC
Fort Collins, Colorado

This work is the copyrighted property of Eugene M. Gagliano and may not be reproduced, scanned, or distributed for any commercial or non-commercial use without express written permission from the author. No alteration of any of the content is allowed. These poems are a product of the author's imagination.

Copyright 2021 by Eugene M. Gagliano. All Rights Reserved.
Cover photo: Hunter Mesa Sunset, Bighorn Mountains, copyright by Paul Prosinski. Used by permission.

Interior photographs by Eugene M. Gagliano.
Edited by Caren Speckner, Claire Shepherd, and Patricia Phillips
Cover design by Deanna Estes, LotusDesign.biz
Interior design by Deanna Estes, LotusDesign.biz

"Summer Remnants" appears in *Blood, Water, Wind and Stone, an anthology of Wyoming writers,* edited by Lori Howe, Sastrugi Press. 2016. Used by permission.

Library of Congress Control Number: 2020931168

ISBN 978-1-942624-71-4
Printed in the U.S.A.

Our books may be purchased in bulk for promotional, educational, or business use. Please contact Crystal Publishing LLC at crystalpublishingllc.biz.

FIRST EDITION

Sometimes tragedy brings people together in unexpected ways and lifelong friendships develop.

I dedicate this book to my friend,
Governor Mark Gordon, who has supported
both my teaching and writing careers for many years.
I have great admiration and respect for this man of
integrity. He appreciates the importance of poetry,
reading and writing, and loves Wyoming as much as I do.
Mark exemplifies the best of Wyoming.

CONTENTS

Section I: Wyoming 1

Section II: Life 29

Section III: Arts 57

Section IV: People 69

Section V: Nature 93

PREFACE

A Wyoming State of Mind weaves a rich emotional tapestry, reflecting the connection of Wyoming's Poet Laureate to not only our state, but the entire spectrum of human emotion. This work of unique breadth offers richly detailed descriptions of the monumental landscapes of our wonderful state, as well as unvarnished examinations of the fragility of life. Gene's poems tug at the heartstrings, finding beauty in universal, relatable subjects that are alternately tragic and uplifting.

I would expect nothing less from a teacher who brought a unique perspective to my two daughters' 2nd grade education. Enthusiasm, understanding, and commitment were the hallmarks of Gene's classroom. These are still the essential ingredients of Gene's poetry — now flavored beautifully with all the spice of a lifetime in Wyoming.

Wyoming Governor Mark Gordon

BREAKIN' THROUGH
WYOMING

A WYOMING STATE OF MIND

Wyoming,
    land of intricate beauty
    formidable mountains carved
    etched in pristine white peaks
    embroidered in dark pine, spruce and fir
    cliffs, giant shards of granite
    powerful, playful waterfalls
    meandering rivers like sleek water serpents
    carpeted in prairies
    and earthen rose, red bluffs and buttes.

Wyoming,
    home to massive moving herds
    of elk, deer and pronghorn
    not unlike those of the plains
    of Africa's Serengeti
    where eagles take flight
    in skies of eternal blue
    and geese formations like arrowheads
    sever the horizon
    and balsam root blossoms
    mirror the sun
    and swaths of lupine
    swallow the foothills
    in a profusion of color.

Wyoming,
    not just a place
    but a state of mind
    where faith guides people
    and hope rises each day
    with the light of dawn
    where "to lend a hand" is exemplified
    and "neighbor" has true meaning
    where pride in state and country
    radiates like solar rays
    and family comes first.

GAGLIANO

BROKEN BLINDS

Broken blinds above my desk
sever the view from my window,
holding me captive,
chained to it by obligations,
a prisoner of my own making,
dissecting the prairie landscape
into equal parts like striped cloth,

     yet unable to contain my fleeting thoughts
     as they filter through the slats
     out into the blue sky

                   free to dream.

WINDS OF WYOMING

The winds of Wyoming
Surf lofty peaks
Of ice-carved cathedrals
Fueling eagle engines

Which glide on thermal updrafts
Over rocky tree line
Into thick forests
And open parks and meadows.

Winds sift through pine needles
Into glacial valleys where
Stoic bull elk and buck deer
Rule immense herds of grazing life.

Wyoming winds filter down
Into plentiful prairies
Of grass and sagebrush
Owned by pronghorn antelope.

Winds shatter the silent deserts
Where wild horses race with it
Tangling and braiding
Their manes and tails.

The winds of Wyoming
Follow the cottonwood-lined rivers
Awaken the trembling aspen
Into waving their leaves goodbye.

The winds of Wyoming are
      Royalty who reign the land.

Written after listening to "Shiloh Ranch, A Wyoming Tone Poem," Steve Reisteter, World Premiere, November 2, 2017 at the Wyoming Arts Summit; Dr. Michael Griffith, Music Director of the University of Wyoming Symphony Orchestra.

GAGLIANO

SIGNS

The yellow of goldfinch
and meadowlark
will flit away
replaced
by the gold of cottonwood
and aspen leaves.

Informal processions of geese
will arc across the sky
forerunners
of winter's cold winds
that will bare
the soul of nature.

TWISTED WIRE

Twisted and barbed
wire stretches
along ridges of folding hills
and prairie fabric
segregating sheep from cattle
defining properties.

Fence lines that parcel Wyoming
mean nothing to nature.
Wind knows no boundaries
nor do hawks or eagles
rabbit, fox or deer.

Weed seeds filter through fences
and insects crawl beneath them.
Grasses snuggle fence posts
worn wooden sentinels
holding wires taut
in rigid ownership.

Seasons taunt fences
with cold-shattering brittleness
and blizzard's drifting snow
or summer's hot, dry breath of dirt and dust.

Defiant floods
ignore fence lines
carry away the soil.
Twisted and barbed
wire owns the land.

    Deed-less nature
    controls it.

SCULPTED OVERNIGHT

In the backyard
a miniature range of
snowy foothills
sculpted overnight
by unforgiving
blizzard wind.

Reaching the edge
of the birdbath
swirled around
ebony green branches
of spruce
and flocked pine boughs
frozen in time.

Rhythmic strokes
of icy contours
make shadowed
blue-gray depths
softened by sparkling
snow crystals.

Delicately creating
wedding-gown
beauty.

| WYOMING

WALTZING WITH THE WIND

Waving
Distant
Like a mirage
Wind turbine generators
Appear
With graceful
Ballerina arms
Delicate, slow-motion dancers
Waltzing with the wind

SOUTHEAST WYOMING

Serpent trains
rhythmically meander
through buttes and mesas
while clusters of rabbitbrush
jostle along the highway
and November tumbleweeds
cartwheel carelessly
across the pavement
into barbed wire fences,

        their final destination.

LATE SUMMER

Blackbirds sift from the sky
swooping over the foothills
like large flakes of pepper
creating waves of breeze
on an August morning.

A tired gray pavement
cracked and worn
by tires and weather
rises toward a red sun
ripening in a smoky horizon.

Three horses with
polished chestnut coats
catch early morning rays
in tangled manes
reflecting back as gold.

Still, like the dried grasses
and sticky gumweed
except for the swoosh
of flocking birds
and an unseen jet
that fades like late summer.

A school bus
passes me by
with a future generation
as the driver waves
to a teacher walking
into his golden years.

Written after my retirement from 34 years of teaching.

FRENCH CREEK ROAD

Early morning
I walk the road
trying to capture the summer
for winter memories.

Cascading drifts of lupine
tumble down a ravine
in purple splashes.

Sunlight illuminates trembling grasses
with halos of light
spires of yucca blossoms
pierce the prairie.

Sea-foam green sage
mingles with yellow clover
scenting the soft breeze.

Sweeping swaths
of blue-winking flax
thread themselves
among the fields.

Hissing irrigation geysers
pulsate over hayfields.
Horses swish tails in rhythm
to the buzzing assault of flies
as swirling cirrus clouds feather the sky
and power lines hum in the wind.

The pungent stench of road kill
interrupts the moment
      a reminder that, like life,
      summer will end.

ALWAYS THE WIND

Wind,
    Always the wind,
        Voice of the prairie
            Tossing and turning
              Taunting and teasing
              Restless, swirling, twirling
              Pushing and shoving
            Master of the land

                    Sifting dust and snow
                      Into cracks and crevices
                      Trespassing barbed wire
                      Slowed by windbreaks
                      Sculpting storm clouds
                      Forming dust devils

Wind,
    Always the wind,
        Voice of the prairie
            Scolding in winter
            Soothing in spring
            Gently caressing
            Angrily tearing
            Master of the land

THE OLD BARN

Once the monarch of the valley
Proud possession of a man
Now worn-weathered boards splintered
Wooden shingles softened by moss
Broken windows–intruder invitations.

A mouse-infested bat dwelling
After decades of sweet rain, silent snow
And sun-scalding dry winds
Foundation decayed like rotten teeth
Embroidered by rampant weeds.

Carelessly abandoned, forgotten
Wretched symbol of decay
Its aching frame now collapsed
Caving into itself like a roadkill deer
Humbled into submission by nature.

PRAIRIE POPCORN

Grasshoppers
Prairie popcorn
Summer's curse
Uninvited guests
Defy fences
Invade my space

Prairie popcorn
Cancer eating
Butchering
Severing leaves
Exposing skeletal stems
Tattering leafy tapestry
Destroying dreams
Spawned by winter catalogs

WYOMING AUTUMN

I hear the fluttering song of
millions of listless leaves
and the swishing sounds
of brittle grasses
whispering in the wind.

I feel the cold breath of autumn
as it teases and tempts
the cottonwood leaves into gold
and frosts the tomato plants
crystal white that blacken
and hang like wet rags.

I watch generation geese
crease the blue-flame skies
passing into time
and memories
like mist lifting silently
into forever.

A WYOMING STATE OF MIND I

WAGON WHEEL

An aged and weathered
Wagon wheel
At the edge of a flower garden
Leans against a house
Entwined by morning glory vines
The color of the Wyoming sky.

Did it once carry
A family's means of survival
In a covered wagon
On a journey of dreams
Over endless dusty miles
Of scorching sun
And taunting winds?

Does it speak
Of the circle of life?
Remember the heartache of despair?
The miles of sacrifice, pain and loss
Death march or freedom's road?

Is it just a nostalgic ornament
Resting after its long journey
Waiting to rot back to earth?
Or is it the symbol
Of strength, faith and courage
Hope for a new generation's vision?

SUMMER REMNANTS

The sky flares an agitated red,
searing flames of scarlet.
Clouds like smoldering embers
simmer in the October sunset,
a silent reminder of
summer's wildfire fury.
Autumn extinguishes
the torch of summer as
black tree skeletons silhouette
the burnt orange horizon,
remnants of nature's fiery temper.

I LEAVE NO TRACKS

Railroad tracks mirror
a state highway
once a dusty road
that runs through fields
carpeted with sun-bleached grasses
and grayish blue hues of sage wood
and mottled yellow rabbitbrush.

Trains like giant necklaces
adorned with tank and boxcars
in brightly painted graffiti
decorate the landscape and
sing with the repetitive music
of wheels and creaking cars.

Power lines copy the tracks' path
electricity threaded through wires
carrying a better life past
weakened fences of bent and missing slats
buildings now boarded up
others open to the mercy of Mother Nature.

Wretched barns and shoddy sheds,
homes, motels, restaurants and gas stations
with broken windows and sagging roofs
worn like thread-bare tires tossed aside
symbols of prosperity gone.

I sail along the highway
to the visual rhythm of delineator posts
ahead a flock of silver-mantled
wind turbine generators spin
breathing in the Wyoming wind
through propeller lungs.

Roadside ravenous ravens
black messengers feast on death.
Unlike many before me,
I leave no tracks,
       nothing tangible,

              Only the exhaust from my vehicle.

YELLOW CLOVER

Driving to Upton,
I see carbon-copy Angus
scattered among green hills
wave-like,
        rolling,
                rolling,
                        rolling into one other.

Cumulus clouds pile up
against the distant horizon
like enormous mushroom pillows;
the faraway Black Hills
loom in darkened shadows.

Fence posts hem
the edges of fields
billowing with yellow clover.
Their sweet scent filters
through open car windows,
perfuming the air,
drowning me in their fragrance.

The distant clover
projects the illusion of
soft spatters of primrose,
a Monet painting.

Reflective ponds
tucked neatly in the landscape
like glass mirrors
echo the sky's blue.

A pioneer cottonwood
stands alone,
a mighty warrior of survival
with gator-skin bark
and gnarled, arthritic limbs
rotting in its own decay
as a meadowlark's piercing call
reminds me to sing.

*Written for fellow poet Nicholas Trandahl
after visiting him in Upton, Wyoming.*

A WYOMING STATE OF MIND I

SNAKE RIVER RAFT TRIP

It swirled in a myriad of blues and greens
Hiding downed pine and spruce skeletons
Massive rocks and boulders, unseen death traps
Beneath cold clear water and brilliant blue sky.

Waves frosted with glistening sunlight
Sandbar fingers draped with rivulets of water
Rock walls eaten away, decayed-like teeth
By swift currents, gouging out rocky cliff terraces.

Ducks bobbed along worn-rock edges
Bald eagles scouted for fish above the river
Stoic mountain guardians waited for their winter cloaks of snow
Early autumn painted maples, dappled shades of orange and red.

Massive tree root systems appeared as crowns
While death-piled trees spoke of raging spring runoff
Bright yellow-stemmed willow flourished along sandbars
Shiny green leaves reflected brilliant glints of sun light.

Two rubber rafts floated for adventure
In a breath-taking gorge of wonder
Bringing family members closer together
Closer to the power and beauty of nature
With the excitement of sharing white water rapids.

Laughter and love: a summer to remember.

PRAIRIE GRASSES

The long drive
caused me to see
the prairie grasses.
Wave upon wave
of light
flitting across
the restless seed heads
rhythmically swaying in the breeze.
A plethora of colors:
muted wine, wheat, summer green,
burnt sienna and umber,
shimmering in the sun.
A natural flowing quilt
of visual pleasure.

A WYOMING STATE OF MIND |

WIND TURBINE GENERATORS

An invasion of colossal
wind turbine generators
appear on the horizon
alien steel-armored
graceful giants
mammoth marvels of technology
wind-driven
twirling in rhythm
an army of
silver-winged sentinels

WINTER'S DEATH

a delineator post cut off
twisted by the hungry steel blade
of a snow-clearing truck

gritty mounds of snow
straddle the side of the county road
melting under the rays
of sunlight stretching ever
higher into lengthening day

rivulets of snowmelt
trickling quickly down the roadside
sand grinding beneath one's feet

green and yellow spikes of yucca
erupting out of the brown
rocky roadside

the first of green blades of grass
emerging from battered prairie foliage
peppered glints of light
from tossed aluminum cans and bottles

a white jack rabbit carcass
riddled by bloodied gashes
from raucous ravens

horse manure perfuming
the death of winter

LIFE

WHEELS OF TIME

The cycle of life begins when
Rolled in the hospital bassinet
Our first set of wheels

Continues at home
With the crib and stroller
The plastic tricycle takes over
Until we're ready for a real one
We outgrow it
And move on to the bicycle
Roller skates, skateboard, motorcycle
Or four wheeler

Our first "set of wheels"
Places us in the car or truck
Maturing into the bus, subway or train
Alas, time finds us using
the motorized shopping cart
the walker, the wheelchair or
the hospital bed

       the wheels of time full cycle

YOU CAN'T SEE LOVE

Love is an emotion
That can't be seen,
Except in acts of kindness.

A child picks a dandelion just for you
Or draws you as a stick figure.
A mother rocks a sick child
In the middle of the night.
A father changes a dirty diaper.

A mother makes your favorite meal.
A father and mother both work
To put food on the table.
Friends plan a surprise birthday party.
Somebody gives a gift "just because."

A boy gives his girlfriend
A box of chocolates, flowers and wine.
Two teens carve their names inside a heart
On a tree trunk or a picnic table.
Friends share a meal.

Two patients lying side by side, prepare
For a kidney transplant.
A friend visits a patient in the hospital.
A Salvation bell-ringer collects money
To help the less fortunate.

An old man pushes his wife in a wheelchair.
An elderly lady bakes cookies for the pastor.
Grandparents hug and kiss grandchildren.
A married couple holds hands.
A family plans a 50th wedding anniversary.

      Love is an emotion
           That can't be seen,
                  Except in acts of kindness.

GAGLIANO

GARAGE SALE

clothing hangs limp
precious gifts
once treasured
reminders
of happier days

tangled tree lights
once bright with hope
sit lifeless

gadgets
once time savers
now three for a dollar

Mom's possessions
soon scattered
only memories left

*In memory of my
beloved mother,
Caroline Gagliano.*

UNWANTED CALL

the phone rings
unexpected
like a bee sting
    stuns, overwhelms
        a tsunami of feelings

the heart severed
by shards of grief
shatters the ordinary
    shocks the body
        spasms into sobs

            crumbling emotional wreckage

                the unwanted call:
                notification of death

FOUR O'CLOCK APPLE

The four o'clock apple
The favorite rocking chair
That always lucky cap
You feel you have to wear.

The pillow that's just right
The favorite Sunday pew
That special brand of perfume
That's only right for you.

The morning cup of coffee
Midmorning cup of tea
A lemon slice in water
Whatever it may be.

Hot chocolate in the winter
Chicken soup to cure a cold
Garlic to stay healthy
All choices I am told.

Well done or medium rare
Served hot or just plain cold
Are these really choices
Or just habits of the old…

THE CROSSES WE BEAR

So often we are unaware
Of crosses other people bear.
The parents of the son now lost
Who paid the price of freedom's cost.

The teen who tried to take his life
To free himself from worldly strife.
The loss of love, of wife and mother
The accident that took a brother.

The person who lives in constant fear
For loved ones living far and near.
The ominous cancer that ceases breath
The heartbreak news of sudden death.

When an innocent baby's life is taken
And a distraught mother's world is shaken
When angry nature spreads its wrath
A precious home caught in its path.

The person caught in drug addiction
The psychopath whose world is fiction.
We must try to be more aware
Of the many crosses people bear.

OUTSIDE THE DOOR

No cure:
Maybe two months.

His words take her breath away.
Her watery eyes and blank stare
Speak the unspoken.

The doctor apologizes
For what he can't do.

Hope leaves the room
As he closes the door.

Outside the door
He trudges down the hall
To his office.

Sits down in his chair,
Covers his face.

Her would-be savior
Crumbles
And shatters into tears.

He is not God.

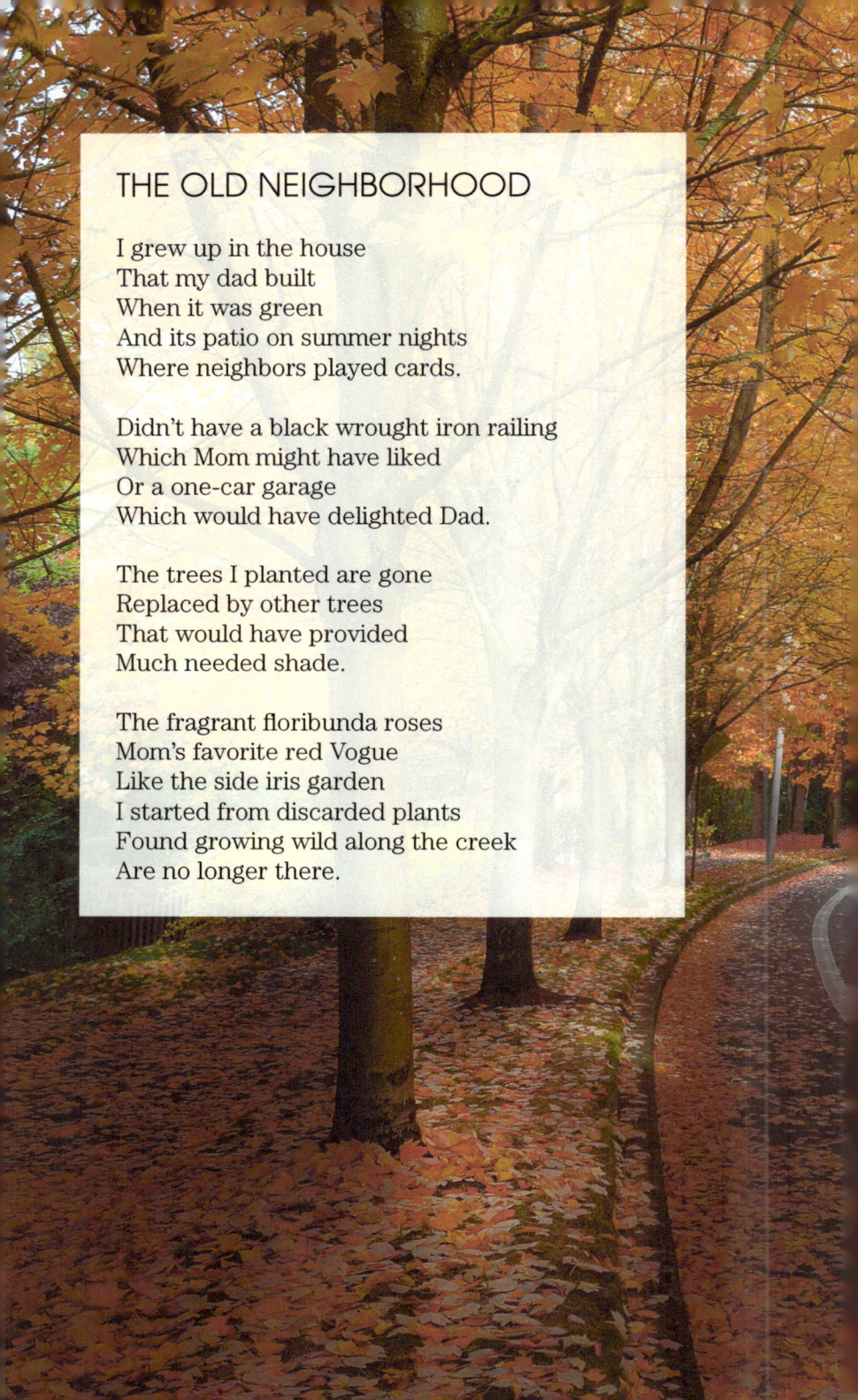

THE OLD NEIGHBORHOOD

I grew up in the house
That my dad built
When it was green
And its patio on summer nights
Where neighbors played cards.

Didn't have a black wrought iron railing
Which Mom might have liked
Or a one-car garage
Which would have delighted Dad.

The trees I planted are gone
Replaced by other trees
That would have provided
Much needed shade.

The fragrant floribunda roses
Mom's favorite red Vogue
Like the side iris garden
I started from discarded plants
Found growing wild along the creek
Are no longer there.

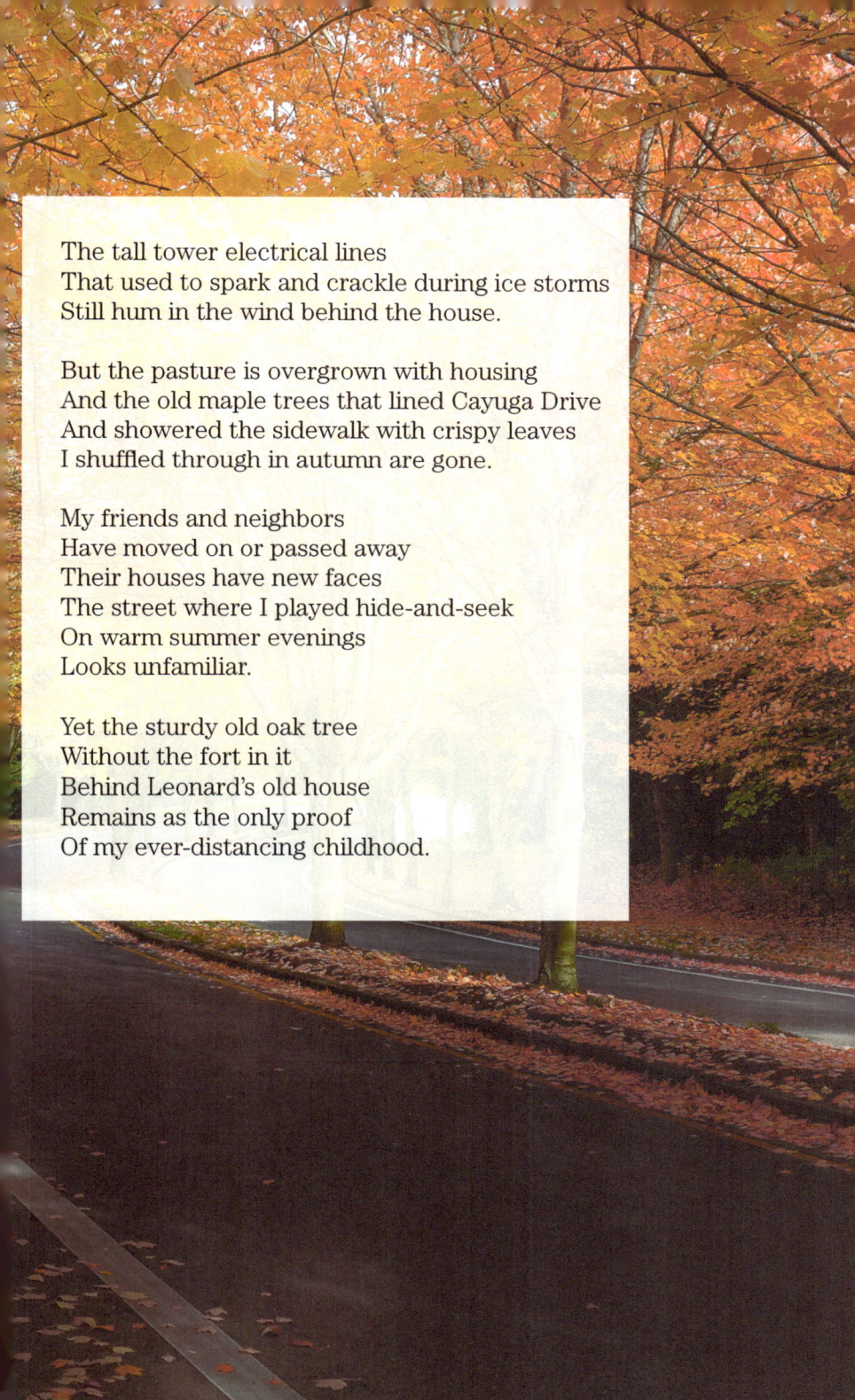

The tall tower electrical lines
That used to spark and crackle during ice storms
Still hum in the wind behind the house.

But the pasture is overgrown with housing
And the old maple trees that lined Cayuga Drive
And showered the sidewalk with crispy leaves
I shuffled through in autumn are gone.

My friends and neighbors
Have moved on or passed away
Their houses have new faces
The street where I played hide-and-seek
On warm summer evenings
Looks unfamiliar.

Yet the sturdy old oak tree
Without the fort in it
Behind Leonard's old house
Remains as the only proof
Of my ever-distancing childhood.

GONE

For sale signs
poke out of
uncared lawns
of houses
once homes
now empty structures
of broken dreams
that shadow the
aging neighborhood
symbolizing the downturn
of a fading economy.

A single trashcan waits for pickup
reminder of another week of summer
like neighbors and friends

                                                  gone…

WILLING TO TRADE

The exterior looks a bit worn, but it has character.
The lighting isn't as bright, but it's still there.
The plumbing can be unpredictable, but it still works.
The wiring's outdated, but it sometimes shorts out.
The frames a little bent, but it's sturdy.
The furnace doesn't work well anymore, but you can insulate.
The curb appeal might be a bit off, but it works.

All in all, it's not a bad deal for anyone willing to trade
        Their body for mine.

UNEXPECTED

On my way to read
That April morning
I stopped for the ambulance
Not knowing, said a prayer.

The phone call came at school
Unexpected, shattered me
Changed his life, our lives.
"Injured on a fire call, emergency room."
The heavy words resounded in my head.

I tried to control the car.
Emotions spewed from my gut.
I raced to see him
Followed the nurse.

Surrounded by grim-faced
Firemen and police
The young man, my son, my baby
Lay blackened, bloodied, but conscious.

I touched his arm, spoke.
Tears blurred my vision.
My wife arrived, stronger than me.
Family and friends came, hugged.
The priest prayed over him.

The doctor took us aside
His words
"Life threatening"
Pierced my heart.

The flight for life arrived.
I kissed his forehead
Told him I loved him.
Cried
As he disappeared
      Into the sky
      Into God's hands.

Written for my son Darin.

I WONDER

A flock of geese
Winged messengers headed north
Harbingers of spring
Fill me with joy.

But
Is it a stronger feeling
Than the sadness
When geese take summer south?

Is having a dream
More wonderful
Than attaining it?

Is the serene soft light of sunrise
More profound
Than the colorful flare of sunset?

Is the ebony stillness of night
Stronger
Than the blackness of depression?

Is the birth of a child
More emotional
Than the death of a loved one?

                                                I wonder…

GRIEF

Grief,
the evil spirit
that destroys the heart
shreds it into shards of despair
severs the arteries of love
trashing the frail filaments of hope
into a web of disbelief
dashing dreams to death
shattering the meaning of existence.

REMEMBER WHEN

Remember when
Clouds and imagination
Created endless possibilities
Of creatures in the sky?

Swinging meant touching the heavens
And never wanting to stop
And there really was gold
At the end of a rainbow?

Remember when
Summer
Took forever to get here
And a lawn sprinkler
Produced hours of fun
And you never wanted
A game of hide-and-seek
To end?

Remember when
You tried to get a glimpse
Of Santa on Christmas Eve
And building a snowman
Was a work of art?

When a wrapped present
Caused great anticipation
And sledding
Was the fastest way to travel?

Remember when
Life was full of simple pleasures?

EVIL

Evil is a riptide
in the ocean of life
a cancer that eats away
at the human soul
like maggots on a corpse.

A tidal wave of death.

PLANT SEEDS

Plant the seeds of prejudice
And hate and anger grow,
Inviting crime and violence
As everyone should know.

Plant the seeds of acceptance
And love and kindness grow,
Inviting trust and friendship
As everyone should know.

FOR MY CHILDREN

Let their conflicts be like summer storms,
    Only there to clear the air.

Let their losses be like autumn leaves,
    Only there to grow on.

Let their burdens be like snow upon the bough,
    Only there to strengthen them.

Let their sorrows be like spring rains,
    Only there to make them grow.

OLD MAN'S CURSE

I'm an old man.
I don't carry a purse,
But sometimes I think
It must be a curse.

Where should I keep
My chapstick and candy,
Inhaler and pill case
So it will be handy?

Where should I put
My wallet and keys,
Cough drops and change?
Lord, help me please.

A pocket can hold
Only so much
Maybe a purse
Should be a crutch.

BROKEN DREAMS

Broken dreams
    Like shards of glass
        Pierce the heart
      And sever
            The arteries of hope
          To the soul.

GOODBYES

Spoken
      whispered
           thought

Goodbyes to childhood innocence
Graduation goodbyes written in yearbooks
Well-intentioned, heartfelt words
"I'll keep in touch," fading all too soon
Like autumn leaves.

Airport goodbyes, bus terminal, train station
Holiday goodbyes to family and friends
Vacation goodbyes with that last glimpse
Of the island, ocean or mountains.
Becoming fond memories like
Dissipating mist in warming sun
Seasonal goodbyes with the certainty they will return.

Goodbyes to parents as young people leave home
To find their place in the uncharted world
Goodbyes to shattered dreams crushed by reality
The last goodbye when placing a rose on a casket.

Goodbyes are beginnings and ends
Goodbyes are the lacerations of life
Piercing the skin of our heart and soul
Leaving unseen scars.

LOVERS' HANDS

Young lovers' hands
Holding on to one another's dreams.

His, strong with purpose, tough yet tender
Hers, delicately smooth and caring, gentle yet strong
Holding each other, gold bands shining
Loving the land, loving each other.

Together building a home, breaking the sod, raising a family
Working partners, friends and lovers.

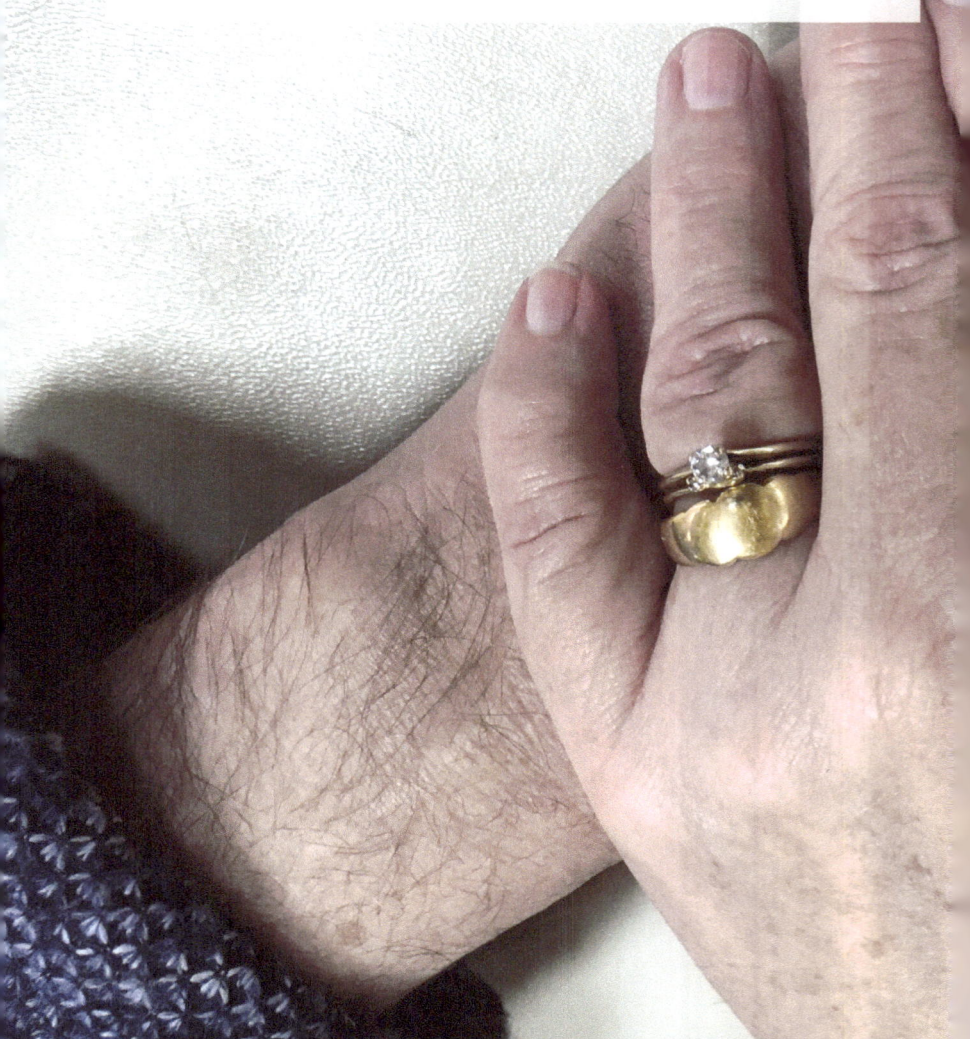

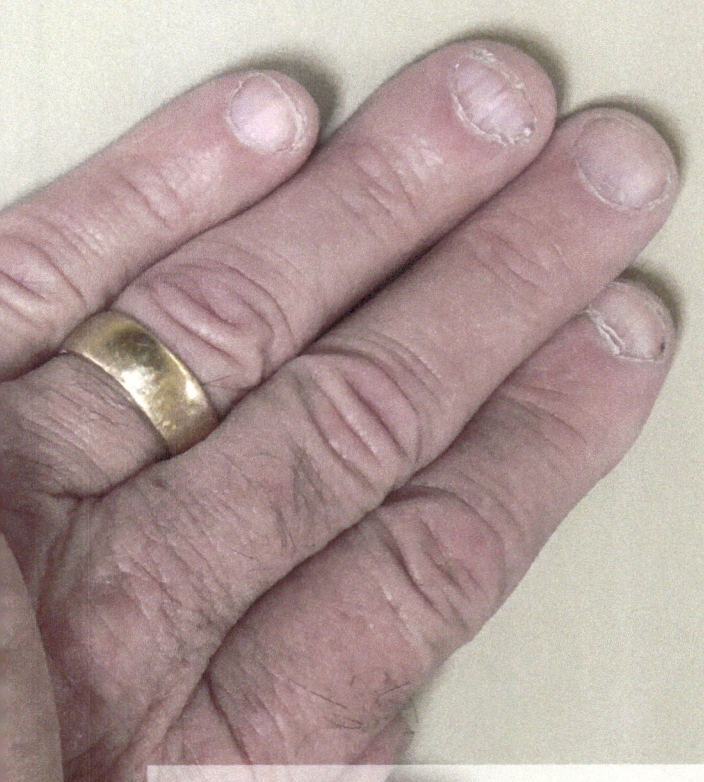

His, planting, building, protecting his own
Hers, washing, cooking, caressing their children
Both nurturing, giving, suffering
Celebrating life, saying goodbye.

Grasping hands, clinging to life
Weathered by wind, oppressive heat and killing cold
Fists clenched in anger, hands raised in prayer
Hands, tired and old, veins bulging
Under skin like dried riverbeds
Fingers stiff and bent.

      Old lovers' hands, gold bands shining
      Still holding on to one another's dreams.

THE ARTS

MUSIC

Music is the universal glue of mankind
a gift that crosses the lines of race, color and creed
celebrates history, heroes, hunger and pain
circles the kaleidoscope of emotions
the tenderness of love, the wrenching heartbreak of sorrow
the melancholy mist of uncertainty
light-hearted humor, the triumphant joy of victory.

Young or old, music lifts our spirit
calms our anxiety, renews our hope
promises, revitalizes, energizes.
Immersed in musical notes
memories swirl from the depths of our being
recycling a festival of feelings.
Song is the voice of the soul taking flight,
and dance, its rhythm.

> Music is a gift to be shared, enjoyed and celebrated.
> Music knows the heart of the world
> and brings us together as one.

VOICE

The ability to take musical notes
from sheet music
to make them leap off the page into song
or retrieve a tune from memory
is a blessing.

I no longer lament that
I can't play piano or trumpet.
My voice is the ultimate instrument
taken anywhere, anytime
to lift the heart, comfort the soul.

My voice can create the mellow sounds
of a cello, the soothing sound of a French horn
or the chirping bird song of a flute.
My voice can raise itself in praise
or make my feet dance.

I can sing a lullaby, a love song,
hymn, country, folk or rock.
The voice that stirs from deep within my soul
has a special beauty of its own.

My voice is a gift to share with many.

THE CONCERT OF LIFE

The Great Conductor

    composed
    the melodies of our lives
    our songs, our stories

    which direct
    the high and low notes
    played out
    by the instruments

The people

    who solo and sing in unison
    with crescendos and decrescendos
    of events
    and the sharps and flats of emotion

The symphony

    with all its tempos
    is the whole world
    with its chorus
    of base, tenor, alto and soprano
    personalities

        who comprise the various themes
        played out in the concert of life

A WYOMING STATE OF MIND I

BRAM BRATA

Under a canopy of maple leaves
On a warm summer evening
A gentle breeze carries
The musical notes
Of a steel drum orchestra
Of teens on a four-day tour
To entertain in the heart of a city park.

Young people, closing the gap of generations
Familiar tunes presented in unique ways
The music ignites fresh life into the crowd.
Young children dance, the elderly are moved
To tap their feet, clap their hands
Heads sway.

The group's energy
Radiating into the hearts
Of life's silver-haired survivors
Remembering forgotten hopes and dreams.
The flicker of youth rekindled
In old eyes of what was or could have been.
The primal beat of the drums,
The heartbeat of the crowd, of life.

Music bonding people.

Written while visiting Karen in Coeur d'Alene, Idaho.

WYOMING'S TAPESTRY OF TALENT

Artists
tell the stories of humanity
in varied creative venues.

Writers craft words to inform and inspire.
Storytellers hold on to our history.
Actors and actresses give life to script
that makes us laugh or cry.

Musicians breathe life into instruments
and singers use their voices to
create music that tugs at the heart
or makes us dance.
Dancers offer visual expression
of music found in the soul.

Artists put paintbrush to canvas
capturing visual slices of life.
Artists use rainbow-colored threads
to sew, knit and crochet
a myriad of detailed patterns.

Potters mold beauty from clay
while photographers
secure precious moments
of life for posterity.

Artists enrich our lives.

GAGLIANO

ART

Art
  the voice of creation
  in all its forms
  helps us
  to see more clearly
  the world wrapped around us
  better understand ourselves
  helps us visualize
  the ordinary in a new light
  opening our minds and hearts

Art
  expresses our deepest thoughts
  the human emotions trapped inside us
  reminds us of who we are
  gives simple pleasures
  captures special moments in life's journey
  fills the innate need for love and beauty

Art is the polished gem of life.

POETS

Some say poets see the world
Through rose-colored glasses
But I think they see it more clearly.

The poet is stirred to express
Life in words
Sensitive to the human condition
Compelled to try
And capture snippets of life
Helps visualize moments
That awaken the heart
Revives memories
Sees in the mirror of truth
The humor in a situation
Creates awareness so often
Overshadowed by daily life.

The poet observes the world
For inspiration
Searches the caverns of the soul
Seeks meaning and understanding
Uses his craft as a gift
To convey inner-most thoughts
And deepest emotions
Strengthens faith
Enables others
To express feelings
They themselves cannot verbalize.

    The poet is not afraid
        To let others look into his soul.

A WEEKEND STAR

I was asked and volunteered
To be in the fundraiser show
For the community hospice
To be Sonny Bono
And sing a song
And do a dialog with Carla.

I spent several weeks
Studying the YouTube video
Observing gestures
And facial expressions
Learning the dialog lines
Memorizing the words to the song.

I ordered a costume online
A Sonny Bono wig
Dragged out my old
White-patent leather boots
Bought makeup to color my eyebrows
And darken my mustache.

I practiced by myself
I practiced with Carla
The week of the show
I rehearsed and rehearsed
Then came the dress rehearsal
I wondered if I could really do it.

| PEOPLE

The night of the first performance
I knew every line of the song and dialog.
The curtain opened
The band began to play.
The spotlight shown bright on us and
Seeing us, the crowd burst into laughter
Carla and I started to sing.

I focused on my parts
Adrenaline took hold of me
I became Sonny
And she became Cher
And for a few brief moments
We became two different people.

We finished our dialog.
The audience cheered and applauded
The stage went dark
The curtains parted for us
I went backstage into the blackness.

                         A dream,
                         I was a star.

Dedicated to Carla Bishop.

FETTUCCINE ALFREDO

Praises for Fettuccine Alfredo should be sung
For that rich creamy sauce upon my tongue.
Pasta drenched in butter and Parmesan cheese,
I'll have another serving, if you please.

Requested by Strahan and Lisa for Good Morning America and read by me on video for National Fettuccine Alfredo Day.

PEOPLE

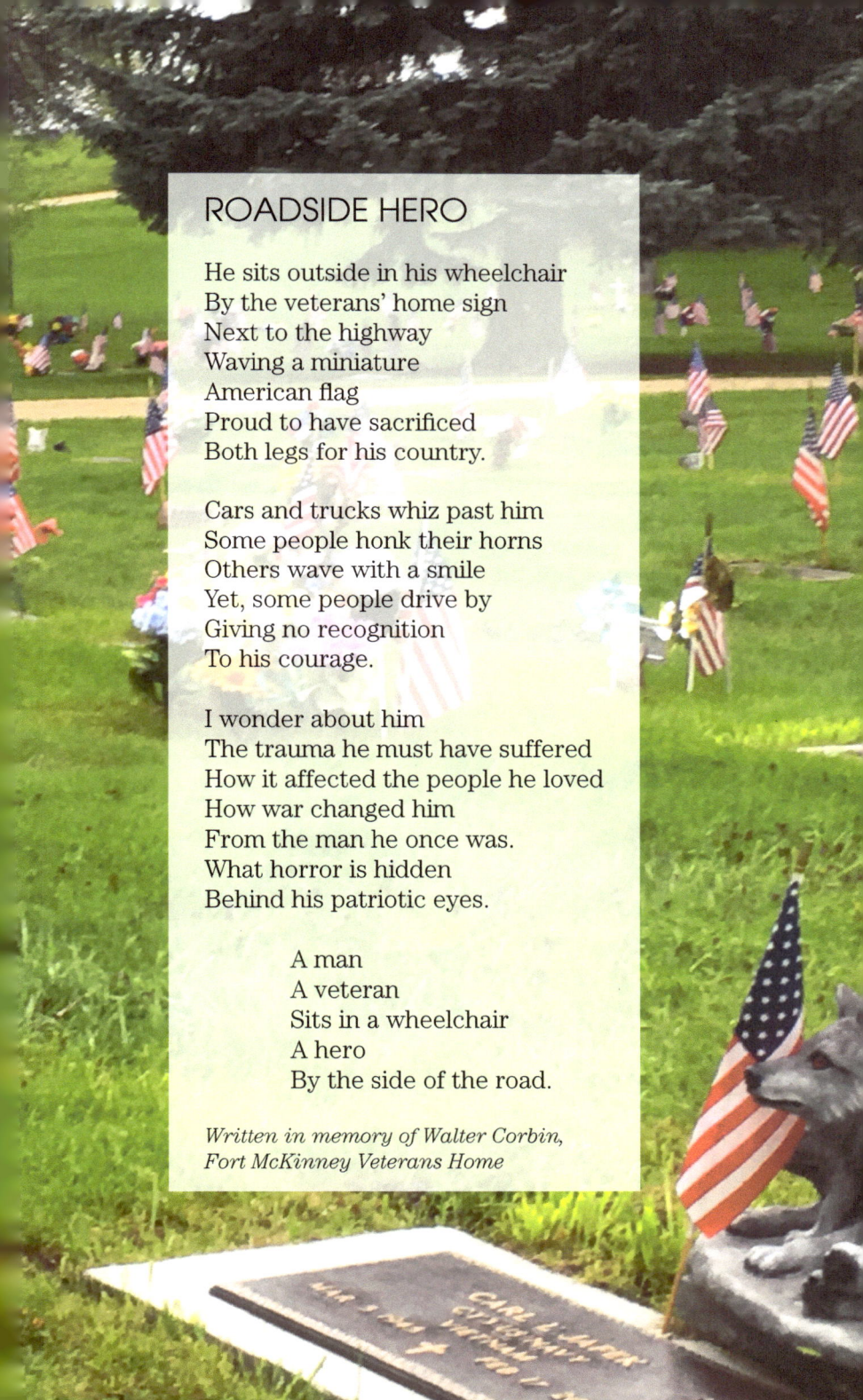

ROADSIDE HERO

He sits outside in his wheelchair
By the veterans' home sign
Next to the highway
Waving a miniature
American flag
Proud to have sacrificed
Both legs for his country.

Cars and trucks whiz past him
Some people honk their horns
Others wave with a smile
Yet, some people drive by
Giving no recognition
To his courage.

I wonder about him
The trauma he must have suffered
How it affected the people he loved
How war changed him
From the man he once was.
What horror is hidden
Behind his patriotic eyes.

    A man
    A veteran
    Sits in a wheelchair
    A hero
    By the side of the road.

Written in memory of Walter Corbin,
Fort McKinney Veterans Home

MOTHER TERESA

The world is in awe
of the tiny
wisp of a woman
now called
Saint Teresa of Calcutta.

Strong in conviction
of God's will for her
strong in prayer
and love of God.

She is a beacon of light
for the destitute
and dying.

Mother Teresa
is an example
of God's love
of what all of us could
and should be.

REMINDERS

I see them at church
Sunday mornings
Dressed up

The silver-haired survivors
Hunched alone in the pews
With their memories
Widows with watery eyes
And trembling lips of prayer
Their parchment hands clasped
Waiting in the flickering candlelight
Listening to hymns that stir their hearts

I see them
These testimonials to love
Reminders of my mother

A BOX OF CRAYONS

He looks up at me from the table,
"Do you want to color?"
"Not today," I answer. "I can't stay."
His face saddens.
"I've got something for you."
His eyes open wide.
I hand him a new box of crayons.
He smiles, toothless, and hurriedly opens the box
And pulls out a yellow crayon.
He draws the sun
And holds up his paper, his eyes searching for approval.
"I like it."
He continues to color, happily humming.
"I need to go to work now."
He doesn't look up, lost in color.
The nurse looks at me and smiles.
"I'll take good care of him."
I touch his shoulder. "Goodbye, Dad."

TWO FRIENDS

Early morning
Two friends
And a golden retriever
Walk the foothills
Of the stringer mountains
Of the Rockies.

Follow the remnants
Of the old Pony Express Trail
Pass among Ponderosa pine
And Douglas fir
Speaking of life
Head toward the horizon
Of the Continental Divide.

Note the harebells'
Dainty blue blossoms
Wild magenta geraniums
And cow parsnips
Bolder than Queen Anne's lace
Soak in the sun's warmth.

Listening to a little stream's cadence
Singing in the dappled shade
Breathing the pine-scented air
Grateful for friendship and nature.

Written for my friend Willy.

MAN'S REFLECTION MIRRORED

I see myself
mirrored
in the reflection
of water
sometimes placid
giving life
nurturing
beautiful
yet at times
turbulent
forceful
destructive.

    I wonder
    if the reflection is real.

THE WALKER

He walks
Daily
Having cheated death
Determined to stay in shape
Though time erodes his youth.

His stride is shorter
Slower
His knees flabby-skinned.

Wrinkled
White-haired
He waves to those who remember him.

Once a prominent community figure
No longer in the limelight
His influence waned
With the loss of his position
Of power and control.

Will he be missed?
      Remembered
      As he thought he would be?

ACKNOWLEDGMENT

A nod, a smile, a wave
A wink, a hug, a kiss
A touch, a handshake, a nudge
A pat on the head or shoulder
Or playful punch in the arm

A caring gesture
A thank you
An opened door
Shared thoughts or candy
A phone call, an email,
Holiday, birthday or
Thinking-of-you card

The human communicators
Acknowledging our presence
Our very existence
Making us feel alive
Important and worthwhile.

KEARNEY, NEBRASKA AIRPORT

I asked the young man
in army camouflage,
Peterson,
where he was going.
Afghanistan.
Shook his hand.
Thanked him
for what he was doing.
Watched him
hug his mother,
pregnant sister, niece and nephew
goodbye.

Watched them cluster by the window,
sister unraveling into tears,
mother consoling, surface strong.
Watched him,
trusting,
walk off into his future.

THE TRUCK CRASH

First on the scene,
The truck lay on its side.
The cab curled into itself
Like a leaf containing spider eggs,
A trail of white liquid behind it.

I cautiously approached,
Fearing death.

Then the calls for help:
A son begging, crying out
In unimaginable pain
For his father to help him.
Screaming, "Get the seat off me!"
My arm! Oh God, I'm going to bleed out."

    Pleading,
        pleading,
            pleading for help.

Looking into the wreckage,
I can barely see them:
Two men trapped.

I started toward my car for my cellphone.
Another driver and his wife approach,

                Call 911.

I tried to lift the seat off him
But couldn't.
The other stranger and I
Tried to lift the seat,
But to no avail.
Anybody have a knife to cut the seatbelt?
A crowbar?
A woman returns with a knife.
The man cut the belt,
I felt utterly helpless.

The father tried to remove
All the debris from his son,
Get closer to help him,
All the while the young man's wailing,

       Pleading,
            pleading,
                  pleading for help.

The father, desperate,
The wreckage cutting into his son's flesh,
Throwing everything he could off his son,
Water bottles, a red notebook, papers, packages of food.
The other man and I helped him.

Repeatedly, I told him help is on the way.
I could only pray over them.
I reached into the cab
Touched the top of his head.
He reached out.

Continued on next page

A WYOMING STATE OF MIND I

I grasped his hand.
He held mine tightly.
"Hang in there. Help is on the way."
He released my hand as his son wailed,
"I can't take it! Help me!"

    Pleading,
        pleading,
            pleading for help.

Another traveler stopped to help
He had a metal cutting saw
Tried to cut through the steel
That kept the young man entrapped.

He used two batteries and stopped,
His arm numb, passed it to the other man.
Sirens, a police car came.
"Ambulance is on its way."
Gathered information from me.
Ambulance arrived
Needed me to move my vehicle.
I left in shock, heavy
Wishing I could have done more.

    Praying,
        praying,
            praying.

LOST

I savor the memories

All that's left
Of a 53-year friendship
That began in college
And couldn't be lost
To the years and miles apart.

Her loss, so personal,
A life once closely shared
Devastation to her family.
She won't have to suffer
Cancer or dementia
A blessing, but to die
The way she did?
Heart-wrenching.

I'll miss the annual
Halloween and Thanksgiving greetings
The Easter card of hopeful rebirth
Of which she's now a part.
The awaited Popcorn Factory canister
At Christmas won't come this year
Or the funny birthday card.

I won't be the shoulder to cry on
Make her laugh, brighten her day
Hear her voice, her New York accent.

       Forever lost, but not forgotten.

Written in memory of my dear friend, Letty.

THE TREE HOUSE

It was a little boy's dream
Or was it?

Built by a father's love
A rustic log cabin
Perched high on wooden stilts
With stairs and a small porch
Two windows and a door
A place for a boy
To dream, imagine
And fantasize
On summer days and
Sleepover nights.

Now weathered and abandoned
Wind-ripped roof at one end
Covered in bird droppings
Log bark worn away
Angled windowpanes hang
A baby rabbit finds refuge in
A wood pile beneath it.

A father and a young man
Stand before this symbol
Of a childhood
The seasons have ended
A time that can never be again.

    It was a little boy's dream
    Or was it?

Written for my son Nathan and grandson Connor.

SHAWN

I tried to encourage him.
He was a good kid,
Likeable, respectful,
With wavy brown hair
And western-blue eyes.

I watched him grow
Alongside my son.
Something about him
Set him apart, a caring demeanor,
Polite, quiet but not shy.

Now an adult, he's
A loving husband and father
With wavy brown hair
Flecked with silver,
His eyes brighter than ever.

His wild side's more subdued,
Yet he continues
To seek peace
In the mountains and wildlife.

A man of compassion, conviction
and understanding,
Adventuresome, a nature-lover
One who appreciates
The smallest gifts of beauty.

Always willing to help
With a smile and a playful side
Intelligent and self-sufficient
At times intense, focused.
He's passionate about his work.

He's a dear friend in my old age
Taking time for me
Encouraging me
Somebody to talk to
Sharing faith, laughter and tears.

Now I watch his son grow
Loving, like him, full of mischief,
Life and energy
A heart like his father's.

       I encourage him.

Written for my friend Shawn.

CHILDREN HELP US SEE

Children make us live again
Let us see
The wonders of life
Enjoy the rain
The colors of the rainbow
The fun of splashing in a puddle.

Children remind us
Of the simple happiness
A new box of crayons
The true anticipation
Of Christmas dreams
And opening a present.

Children remind us
Of the simple joys of life
Flying a kite
Chasing bubbles
Savoring ice cream
Toasting marshmallows.

Children remind us
Of the magic of a colorful balloon
The happiness of a carousel ride
The longing to swing higher
Help us stretch our imaginations
Warm our hearts with their innocence.

Children make us live again
Let us see
The wonders of life
Puppies and kittens
The comfort of a simple hug
The joy of trust, holding a hand.

        Children help us see.

SECOND GRADERS

Second graders,
Little children with little hands,
Reaching out to me.
Curious, open minds with
Bright-eyed stares
And trusting hearts
Looking to me
For help and answers.

Second graders,
Human clay ready for sculpting
With praise and reassurance,
Full of big ideas and promises.
Centers of the world
So easily destroyed.
Enthusiastic creators
Coloring and painting.

Second graders,
Social outcasts picking their noses,
Wearing lunch on their sleeves
Running everywhere
With untied laces
Missing front teeth and tousled hair
The loveable and huggable
Promises of the future.

FAMILY

Family,
    an intricate web of people
    covered by a canopy of unconditional love
    acceptance and affection
    complicated by individual temperaments
    emotions, love and hate, joy and grief
    different hopes and dreams
    personal agendas and expectations.

Family,
    an emotional whirlpool of pride
    pet peeves and hurts
    envy, anger and jealousy
    decades of birth and birthdays
    worship
    weddings and anniversaries
    divorce
    graduations, diplomas, promotions
    accidents, disease, recovery and death.

Family,
    generations
    sharing times of joy
    smiles, hugs and kisses
    sharing times of sadness
    misfortune and loss
    supporting, crying and embracing.

Family,
    a foundation
    for many who are one.

Written for the Fera family.

NATURE

STARTLED BY NATURE

I was startled

> by a feathered explosion
> of hundreds of blackbirds
> that shattered
> like a windshield
> the soft-melon
> morning sky
> then spattered sparks of ebony
> among the field
> of dying grasses.

I was startled

> by a pronghorn
> and twin fawns
> that flitted across the meadow
> scattering rabbits
> that skittered
> alongside the road
> evidence of exploding populations
> due to spring moisture
> and plentiful forage.

I was startled

> by the smoke-tainted horizon
> which whispered of
> western fires burning death
> devouring forests
> making way for new life
> setting the stage for
> spires of purple fireweed
> to spotlight themselves
> amidst black skeletal trees.

I was startled by nature.

DEATH CREATES NEW LIFE

Flowers die and produce seeds
That will grow into new flowering plants.
Forest fires force Lodgepole pine cones
To burst forth their seeds
Which allow natural reforestation by new seedlings.
Scarred, burned areas foster flames of purple flowering fireweed.

Trees die, fall, rot and become logs,
Homes for ants and insect larvae,
A source of food for birds, bears and other creatures.
Decaying leaves and other plant vegetation
Enrich the soil for new trees and plants.
Salmon spawn and die to give life to fry.

Death creates new life.

WINTER ROSES

Winter roses flower differently.

They appear at dawn
As tissue paper-like clouds
Part the curtains of darkness and light
Offering another day.

They frost the mountain peaks
In shades of suffused pink
And flit at the feeder
As rosy finches and Redpolls.

Winter roses blossom
Among the dried grasses
In shale and scoria.

They show themselves in windows
Reflecting the sun's
Early morning rays
Shimmering on placid pond water.

Winter roses have no scent
But warm us with their color.

SUMMER WALK

Strands of clouds shatter the sun into an omelet of orange.
Fences mend meadows and pastures together
With blue flax-spattered pieces of sky.
Ancient cottonwoods with trunks like wrinkled elephant skin
And leaves like shimmering green coins
Glisten in the early morning sun.

Sweet-scented yellow clover billows with humming bees
As twin fawn pronghorns prance over a hill.
A swollen creek rushes to grow wider.
Black Angus bulls bellow in the distance.
A friend heads to town with the burden of his son's loss
As passing pickup trucks and cars swish by
Some trailing the rancid smell of diesel fumes.
Pulsating surges of irrigation lines make rainbows
While an old iron wheel rusts into eternity.

My panting dog happily sniffs her way into the new day
As salty sweat seasons my upper lip.
Ripening stems of cheatgrass
Silently steal the green of summer.
The sickening stench of road kill rises
With the sun as it stretches toward noon.

| NATURE

THE BLUE RIDGE MOUNTAINS

Visitors seek peace and beauty in the vast forest of autumn.

Black balsam fir etch against a burning cobalt horizon
And cherry red sour gum trees tuck themselves
Among the mountain landscape
Of feathery green hemlock and yellow-orange maple.

Waterfalls cascade threads of diamond droplets
Sliding and gliding down slippery slopes of shimmering granite.
Wispy webs of clouds weave between gently carved coves.

Cyclical seasons and weather continue to shape
The Blue Ridge Mountains of North Carolina
As the passage of time molds the lives of old college friends
Traveling together, reminiscing and making new memories
For the autumn of their lives.

Written for Bob and Joanne Gance of Asheville, North Carolina.

SERPENT STREAM

The serpent stream slithers
Through the valley floor.

    Winding,
        winding,
            winding

Sliding stealthily among its banks
Carving and carrying away sediment.

            Swirling,
        swirling,
    swirling

Scurrying among the rocks
Swerving around the boulders.

    Rushing,
        rushing,
            rushing

Endlessly searching for the unknown
Unbridled energy enjoying its freedom.

            Seeking,
        seeking,
    seeking

The serpent stream slithers
Through the memories of my mind.

THE OLYMPIC BEACHES

We're drawn to the Olympic coast
to the beaches
where tides recycle endless waves
and sea birds dance to the rhythmic
beat of winged flight
as mist sifts among sea stacks
and wet stones glitter
like jewels on the sand
among the patterned footprints
of birds and people.

We stand on cliff tops
watching the churning surf
and bleached beach logs
once towering rainforest trees
now forsaken monarchs.

Young lovers hold hands
dreaming of the future.
And old couples arm-in-arm
remember the past.
Children splash in wonder
collecting shells and stones
building sandcastles.

We try to capture the beach
collecting memories
in shells, pictures and paintings.
We're drawn to the ocean
where thoughts drift beyond the water
seeking answers, understanding and truth.

A WYOMING STATE OF MIND I

UNGRATEFUL FURY

Stormy, dark, angry
Self-centered clouds
Puff up with weathered pride

Argue who is largest, strongest
Strike each other with flashing
Jagged electrical swords

Raise jealous voices
In thunder that
Booms, crackles and rumbles

Hurl rain and hail
With blinding fury
Flaunting uncontrolled winds

Lifting, tearing and ripping
Raging destruction and heartache
Without concern or pity

Ungrateful
To the very earth
That spawned them

| NATURE

LIFE AND DEATH

Water is the essence of life,
Gentle like spring rains or mist,
Strong like rapids and waterfalls.

Fluid, water trickles, sprays, spatters,
Gurgles, rushes, plunges and carves.
Water creates rainbows and reflections.

Water has a music all its own
With rhythmic splashing waves and bubbling streams
Or roaring surf, flashfloods and tsunamis.

Water is a raindrop, a stream, a creek, a river,
A puddle, a pond, a lake, a sea, an ocean,
A bead of sweat, a tear.

Water sustains life
And destroys it.
Water: life and death.

CONDEMNED

flatulent clouds explode
against my pleading and prayers

thunder snow
heavy, wet, white
egged on by insolent winds

crushing, wrenching, burying
innocent petals and
unsuspecting limbs

destroying years of labor
hopeful dreams smashed
like the brassy trumpets of
bludgeoned daffodils

the helpless gardener
grieves its mortality
condemned by nature

TENACIOUS

Like a seed implanting itself
between a narrow asphalt crack
or a pine tree growing out of a rock,
man's will to live is tenacious.

Like alpine flowers
beneath winter's death-like grip
patiently awaiting spring,
man's desire to overcome is real.

Like mountain goats defying cliffs
or peaks enduring bitter winds
or rivers carving canyons,
man's wish to control is strong.

SCATTERED BONES

Like broken bones
Appearing lifeless
Tree skeletons
Lay scattered
On the forest floor.

Once strong and tall
Tree trunks rot
Returning to earth
Food and sanctuary
For smaller life forms.

Brittle from decay
Branches break down
Giving back sunshine
And rain to the soil
New life from death.

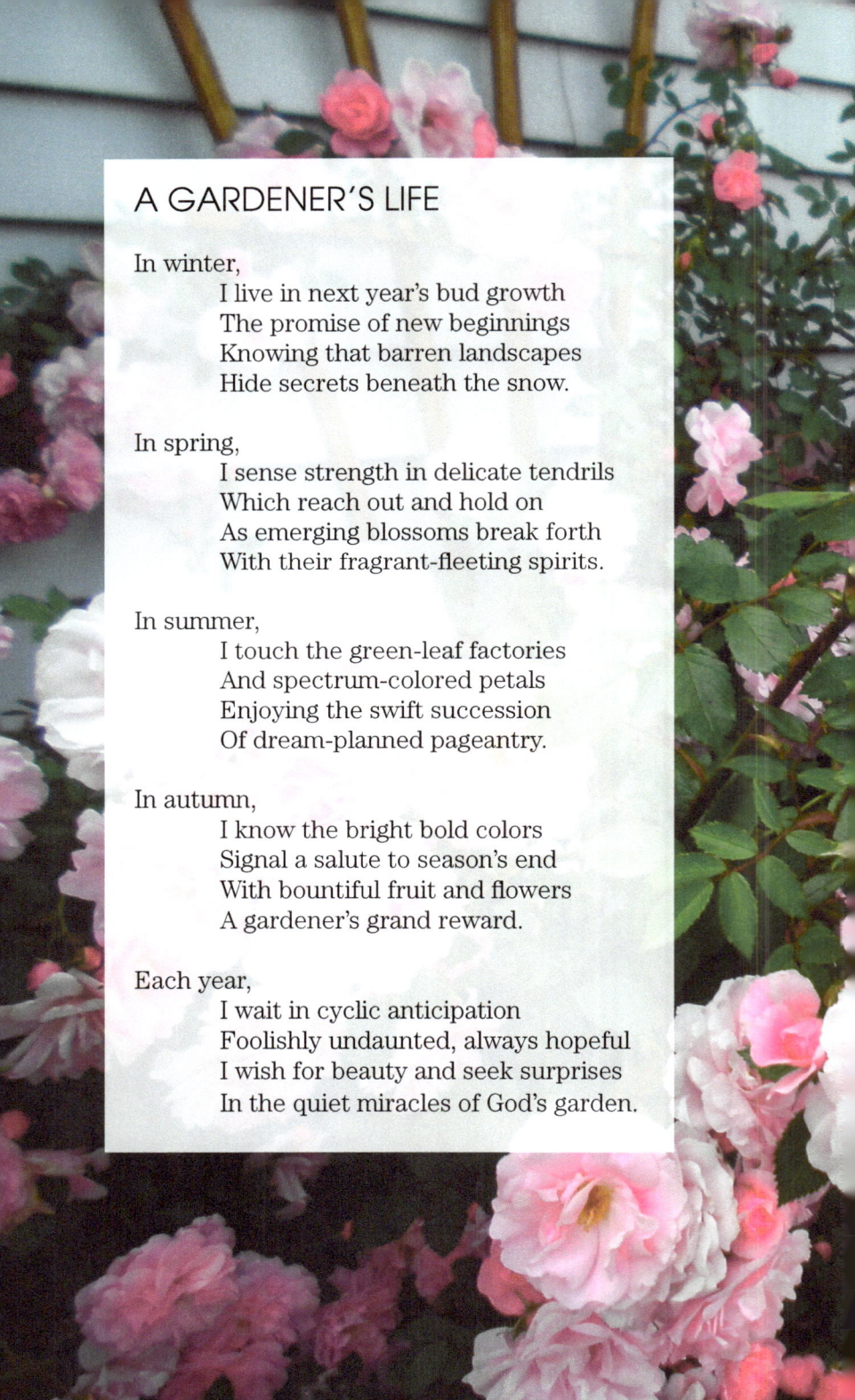

A GARDENER'S LIFE

In winter,
    I live in next year's bud growth
    The promise of new beginnings
    Knowing that barren landscapes
    Hide secrets beneath the snow.

In spring,
    I sense strength in delicate tendrils
    Which reach out and hold on
    As emerging blossoms break forth
    With their fragrant-fleeting spirits.

In summer,
    I touch the green-leaf factories
    And spectrum-colored petals
    Enjoying the swift succession
    Of dream-planned pageantry.

In autumn,
    I know the bright bold colors
    Signal a salute to season's end
    With bountiful fruit and flowers
    A gardener's grand reward.

Each year,
    I wait in cyclic anticipation
    Foolishly undaunted, always hopeful
    I wish for beauty and seek surprises
    In the quiet miracles of God's garden.

WILD ROSES

I see wild roses
From my office window
Tissue-paper petals
Simple pink perfection.
I let them grow
Uncultivated
Special gifts of nature.

Fragrant, tough, resilient
Precious
After the yoke of winter.
Pioneer women must
Have treasured every blossom
The prairie provided.

Perhaps I will request
Wild roses be planted
On my grave site.
Reliable, low maintenance
A promise of hope
Each spring
A reminder.
Love does not die.

FLOWERS

The lilies' white is bursting
The daffodil trumpets play
The bluebells ring their tinkling tune
As the sunrise heralds day.

The asters' shredded beauty
The mums in a crest of gold
The velvet petals of roses
Are beginning to unfold.

Written for Mrs. Erwin, my seventh-grade English teacher.
My very first poem published in the school paper.

A YELLOW CROCUS YAWNED

An abundance of dreams in tiny buds
Began to unfold before my eyes
Then spring kissed the blossoms
And a yellow crocus yawned.

The honeysuckle in green-leaf down
Seemed hushed by the springtime sun
As tulips burning in their beds
Awakened shy, young daffodils.

The golden-armed forsythia
Waved its last farewell
As the shadow of winter
Became lost in the light of spring.

DAFFODILS

Daffodils,
        Slender-leaved soldiers of triumph
        Surge through the warmed mantle of earth
        Beckoning beauty to unfold.

Daffodils,
        Dainty bridesmaids of spring
        Yellow-trumpeted heralds of rebirth
        Golden guests of the sun.

Daffodils,
        Delicate dancers of the wind
        Ballerinas of the breeze
        Petaled butterflies of joy.

CURVES

Curves beckon us
    around the bend
       over the hill
          under the bridge
             beyond the horizon.

             Curves soften our world
              railroads and highways
              foothills and shorelines
                the moon and sun
              flowers and leaves.

        Curves bend for us
       rainbows and rivers
       wheels and wells
      smiles and frowns
    arches and bridges.

LESSON OF THE TREES

Like others
I follow the path
listening to the cadence
of an icy-shackled stream
imprisoned by winter.

Gazing upward,
I see twisted limbs
intricately intertwined
like human lives,
offered up by gnarled trunks
in rippled-patterned bark.

Trees baring their scarred souls
in shades of shadowy light
Undaunted, like people
worn by life,
yet reaching for the sky.

Teaching me to be strong
in my final season.

BREATH OF SPRING

Manmade meteorites
sever the cobalt sky
stitching the pieces together
with soft white strands of floss.

Cumulus clouds collect
creating phantom creatures above
meadows molting their winter skins.

Spring swords of grass
are winning the battle
against wheat-colored stalks
of last season's grass
which are unwilling
to give up their control
over the land.

Queen's cup, tiny white
explosions of beauty
silently emerge along the roadside.

Vehicles pass with carefree waves
as warm winds
breathe new life
into my winter-weary soul.

EUGENE M. GAGLIANO
Poet Laureate of Wyoming

Known by many as "the teacher who dances on his desk," Eugene M. Gagliano (pronounced Galiano) is a retired elementary teacher whose author presentations are entertaining, informative, and inspirational. He has presented at 175 schools; at IRA and SCBWI conferences; and for teachers, libraries, and festivals in Wyoming, Colorado, Missouri, South Dakota, Minnesota, Montana, Nebraska, Texas, and Hawaii.

Gene was the recipient of the IRA's 2004 Wyoming State Celebrate Literacy Award and the 2001 Arch Coal Teacher Achievement Award. Gene's book *Dee and the Mammoth*, illustrated by Zachary Pullen, won the 2010-2011 Wyoming State Historical Society Award for Best Fiction. *Dee and the Mammoth* represented the state of Wyoming at the National Book Festival in Washington, D.C in 2011. His book *Is It True?* was selected as the State of Wyoming's Best Read for 2018 for the National Book Festival in Washington, D.C.

Gene has written the words and music for his song, "Wyoming, It's My Home."

He is a graduate of the Institute of Children's Literature, is a member of Western Writers, Society of Children's Book Writers and Illustrators, International Literacy Association, Wyoming Writers, Wyoming Poets, Johnson County Arts & Humanities Council, Friends of the Library, and is on the Wyoming Arts Council Artists Roster. Gene is the Wyoming State Poet Laureate.

ACKNOWLEDGMENTS

Amazing how a wisp of an old woman, a middle school English teacher, sparked the fire that ignited my poetry career. I am eternally grateful to Mrs. Erwin.

Special recognition goes to my friend, Mike Scarlett, who read the manuscript before I sent it to my publisher, and made me feel very good about myself as a poet and the possibility of publication.

Thanks to Patricia Landy and her husband Ron Phillips of Crystal Publishing for appreciating my work and believing in me. Patricia, working with you was a joy! Your meticulous editing and creativity made this book a stand out. Thanks also to Torrington editor Caren Speckner and Claire Shepherd for their expert editing input. Thanks to Deanna Estes for her great designing talent and Paul Prosinski for the brilliant cover photo.

Then there's my college roommate and lifelong friend, Jim Keough, who always told me, "Come on, Louie, you can do it." Along the way, there have been many people who continued to encourage me to write, college friends like Letty Kopper (deceased) and Bob and Joanne Gance, two of the kindest and most caring people I know. Friends like George and Chris Schafer, who are always there for me, Chuck and Marian Rinn, and Terry and Lynn Ridgeway. Reverend Peter Johnson, Shawn Sullivan, Mary Rhoads, John Snyder, Jerry Harvey, and Gerry Chase are always willing to read my poetry, while Dr. Dozier and Nancy Tabb provide personal, private poetry readings in their home. My chiropractor and good friend, Jimmy Johnson, reads my work, adjusts my neck, and helps me keep a positive attitude. I can never forget, Bill Clark, when during one of my darkest hours, he reignited that spark to write.

Many thanks to all my students over the years who were the source for much of my children's poetry and the staff at Meadowlark School who supported my dream of becoming a writer, especially Joyce Tyrrell, Sherry Tavegie (deceased), Carol Ruby, Kathy Smith, and principals Kathy Camino and Bob Tyser, as well as librarian Claire Johnson (deceased). My former student,

A WYOMING STATE OF MIND I

Mr. Farris, continues to appreciate my work and allows me to share my writing with his students.

What would I have done without my technical supporters, people like Sandy Jelly? Somebody you can count on, who typed my first published book because I'm a lousy typist. Rick Sanchez guided me through many tough spots learning to use my computer, as well as former student, Beau Fowler. More recently, Julie Snyder, who generously gives of her time, has saved the day with her knowledge and computer skills. Colleen Cosner makes me look good for publicity photographs. Mark Bentley, Mark Wilson, and Brady Safranek receive credit for enjoyable interviews that help keep the public informed of my latest endeavors.

Tons of thanks to the Wyoming Poets organization that supports me and other poets like me with writing workshops and places to publish poetry. Special thanks to Wyoming poets like Pat Frolander, Rose Hill, Nick Trandahl, Chris Valentine, Art Elser, Echo Klaproth, and Susan Mark for their inspiration. Much appreciation to writing groups like Third Thursday of Sheridan and Prairie Pens of Gillette for their support. Wyoming Writers, a caring and encouraging group of writers, has been instrumental in sending me out on my writing journey. They taught me to believe in myself.

Children's authors, Bruce Coville and Will Hobbs, always encourage me as a writer, and Aaron Linsdau believes in my children's poetry.

Much gratitude goes to former Governor Matt Mead for selecting me to represent the state of Wyoming as Poet Laureate. People like Michael Lange, Mary Billiter, and Rachel Clifton from the Wyoming Arts Council have been very generous in providing me opportunities to read my work and share my knowledge of writing.

Several Wyoming bookstore owners deserve credit for promoting me as a writer and selling my books: Robby from Sheridan Stationary; Vicki from Wind City, Casper; Jane and Dale from Teacher's Corner; and Sue McBride from Whistle-Stop Mercantile.

It seems trite to say what would I do without the love and support of my wife, Carol, of 49 years, but it's true. Friends say she must be a saint. My children and their spouses—Gina and Ron, Jared and Mandy, Darin and Allison, and Nathan and Lisa lend support, encouragement, and laughter to my life. My family is my greatest blessing in life, and I love them all.